TEXAS TEST PREP

Practice Test Book

STAAR Reading

Grade 6

ISBN 978-1467933759

CONTENTS

Section 1
Reading Mini-Tests

INTRODUCTION TO THE READING MINI-TESTS
For Parents, Teachers, and Tutors

How Reading is Assessed by the State of Texas

The STAAR Reading test assesses reading skills by having students read passages and answer reading comprehension questions about the passages. On the STAAR Reading test, students read 6 to 7 passages and answer a total of 48 multiple-choice questions.

About the Reading Mini-Tests

This section of the practice test book contains passages and question sets similar to those on the STAAR Reading tests. However, students can take mini-tests instead of taking a complete practice test. Each mini-test has one passage for students to read. Students then answer 8 questions about the passage.

This section of the book is an effective way for students to build up to taking the full-length test. Students can focus on one passage and a small set of questions at a time. This will build confidence and help students become familiar with answering test questions. Students will gradually develop the skills they need to complete the full-length practice test in Section 3 of this book.

Reading Skills

The STAAR Reading test given by the state of Texas tests a specific set of skills. The full answer key at the end of the book identifies what skill each question is testing.

There are also key reading skills that students will need to understand to master the STAAR Reading test. The answer key includes additional information on these key skills so you can help the student gain understanding.

STAAR Reading

Mini-Test 1

Instructions

Read the passage. The passage is followed by questions.

Read each question carefully. Then select the best answer. Fill in the circle for the correct answer.

The Lighthouse

Simon was fascinated with the lighthouse to the south of the island. It was just two miles from his front door. The lighthouse stood proudly above the sea and cast its light for miles. At night it was an eerie presence. Simon and his friends were scared to even go near it. One night, Rick was staying at Simon's house.

"I think we should head over there," said Rick, who was Simon's best friend. He was always more adventurous than his sensible friend.

Simon thought carefully before responding.

"But aren't you scared?" he asked.

"Not at all. Are you?" Rick replied.

Simon did not want to look scared in front of his best friend.

"No," he replied nervously.

"That is settled then," said Rick. "We will head out this evening."

After dinner, they gathered some food and supplies and packed them into Rick's backpack. Then they headed out towards the lighthouse. Both boys were very quiet as they walked through the fields on the island.

"You're not saying much," said Simon. "Are you okay?"

"I'm fine," said Rick. "I was just thinking."

When they reached the shore, the sun was starting to set above the sea. The boys slowly climbed the small rock face as the sun went down. They both stopped as they stood in front of the lighthouse door.

"In you go then Simon," said Rick, gesturing towards the wooden door.

"You go first," said Simon. "It was your idea."

Rick paused and didn't say a single word. Then Rick edged towards the door. He was very nervous and unsure. He arrived at the step and reached out towards the door handle. Simon had stayed back in the shadows. As Rick twisted the handle, he suddenly heard a loud growling from inside.

"Run!" shouted Rick at the top of his voice.

He raced away, with Simon following close behind him. They ran towards the main road and headed back towards Simon's house. Rick looked very sheepish as they made their way home.

"Didn't you want to see inside?" asked Simon.

Rick shrugged and looked down at the ground.

"I guess it was scarier than I thought," he whispered.

"Oh, I don't know," said Simon. "It wasn't that bad."

1   Read this sentence from the passage.

At night it was an eerie presence.

Which word means about the same as <u>eerie</u>?

Ⓐ   Welcoming

Ⓑ   Calming

Ⓒ   Creepy

Ⓓ   Noticeable

2   Read this sentence from the passage.

Then Rick edged towards the door.

The word <u>edged</u> shows that Rick moved –

Ⓐ   swiftly

Ⓑ   slowly

Ⓒ   suddenly

Ⓓ   smoothly

3   Which statement is most likely true about Rick?

    Ⓐ   He is not scared of anything.

    Ⓑ   He is more scared than he lets on.

    Ⓒ   He likes seeing how scared Simon is.

    Ⓓ   He only pretends to be scared.

4   Read this sentence from the passage.

> **The lighthouse stood proudly above the sea and cast its light for miles.**

Which literary device is used in the sentence?

    Ⓐ   Personification, giving objects human qualities

    Ⓑ   Hyperbole, using exaggeration to make a point

    Ⓒ   Simile, comparing two items using the words "like" or "as"

    Ⓓ   Symbolism, using an object to stand for something else

5   Why does Rick tell Simon to run?

   Ⓐ   He sees a creature inside the lighthouse.

   Ⓑ   He hears a noise from inside the lighthouse.

   Ⓒ   He thinks they are going to get in trouble for being inside the lighthouse.

   Ⓓ   He realizes that the owner of the lighthouse is home.

6   What is the point of view in the passage?

   Ⓐ   First person

   Ⓑ   Second person

   Ⓒ   Third person limited

   Ⓓ   Third person omniscient

7   How is Simon different from Rick?

  Ⓐ   He is more sensible.

  Ⓑ   He is more adventurous.

  Ⓒ   He is more intelligent.

  Ⓓ   He is more creative.

8   Read this sentence from the passage.

Rick shrugged and looked down at the ground.

  The author uses this description to suggest that Rick feels –

  Ⓐ   angry

  Ⓑ   embarrassed

  Ⓒ   amused

  Ⓓ   terrified

STAAR Reading

Mini-Test 2

Instructions

Read the passage. The passage is followed by questions.

Read each question carefully. Then select the best answer. Fill in the circle for the correct answer.

Mark Zuckerberg

Mark Zuckerberg is a web site developer and computer programmer. He is also a businessperson. He is best known for creating the web site Facebook. Facebook is a web site that allows people to connect with friends and family. He is now the CEO and president of the company.

© Guillaume Paumier,
Wikimedia Commons

Zuckerberg founded the web site in 2004 with some of his Harvard University classmates. He has since overseen the development of the site. Facebook became the most visited online web site throughout 2010. This was also the year that Mark Zuckerberg was named as Person of the Year by *Time Magazine*.

Mark Zuckerberg was born in White Plains, New York in 1984. His early education was spent at Ardsley High School. This was followed by Phillips Exeter Academy. While at Phillips Exeter Academy, he won prizes for his work in science, mathematics, astronomy, and physics. His outdoor pursuits included fencing, and he was captain of the college fencing team. He is also multilingual and can speak French, Latin, Hebrew, and Ancient Greek.

Zuckerberg first showed an interest in computers during middle school. At this time, he started to write software programs. His father hired an experienced software developer, David Newman, to tutor his son. He was identified at this young age to be an amazing talent. This encouraged him to take a graduate course in software design while at high school. He continued to develop computer programs as he learned.

Zuckerberg's main interest was in software that helped people to interact and communicate. This passion inspired a program called ZuckNet. This allowed a small set of users to communicate by 'pinging' each other. It was like a basic version of today's instant messenger tools. Zuckerberg continued to experiment with different software programs. Then he enrolled at Harvard University. During this time, he focused on creating software that connected people through common interests. The inspiration for Facebook came from paper-based books at the university. The books were known as facebooks and showed students' names, photographs, and gave information about them.

Facebook was launched on February 4, 2004. At first it was only for Harvard University students. It soon spread to other major universities including Stanford, Columbia, Yale, and MIT. This was followed by a spread to most universities in the United States. In 2005, it was made available to high schools. This was followed by allowing people from large companies like Apple and Microsoft to join. In 2006, it was made available to anyone over the age of 13. The site has grown rapidly since then. Facebook now has over 500 million users, in hundreds of countries worldwide.

Mark Zuckerberg has developed many different programs to make Facebook more popular in the last several years. These include games, applications, and advertising tools. He is expected to expand the site even further in the coming years.

1   Read this sentence from the passage.

> **During this time, he focused on creating software that connected people through common interests.**

As it is used in the sentence, what does the word <u>common</u> mean?

Ⓐ   Ordinary

Ⓑ   Everyday

Ⓒ   Shared

Ⓓ   General

2   Read this sentence from the passage.

> **He is also multilingual and can speak French, Latin, Hebrew, and Ancient Greek.**

What does the prefix in the word <u>multilingual</u> mean?

Ⓐ   Many

Ⓑ   Early

Ⓒ   One

Ⓓ   Language

3   According to the passage, which of these groups were the first to be allowed to join Facebook?

Ⓐ   University students

Ⓑ   Employees of large companies

Ⓒ   High school students

Ⓓ   Harvard University professors

4   This passage is most like –

Ⓐ   a biography

Ⓑ   an autobiography

Ⓒ   a short story

Ⓓ   a news article

5   Which paragraph has the main purpose of describing how Mark Zuckerberg developed his computer skills?

Ⓐ   Paragraph 1

Ⓑ   Paragraph 2

Ⓒ   Paragraph 3

Ⓓ   Paragraph 4

6   Which sentence from the passage best shows that Facebook is successful?

Ⓐ   *Facebook is a web site that allows people to connect with friends and family.*

Ⓑ   *Facebook became the most visited online web site throughout 2010.*

Ⓒ   *Facebook was launched on February 4, 2004.*

Ⓓ   *This was followed by allowing people from large companies like Apple and Microsoft to join.*

7   Why did Mark Zuckerberg's father most likely hire a software developer to tutor his son?

    Ⓐ   He was worried that Mark was making mistakes.

    Ⓑ   He saw that Mark had a talent worth developing.

    Ⓒ   He saw that Mark was struggling with his studies.

    Ⓓ   He wanted Mark to develop useful programs.

8   The web below summarizes information from the passage.

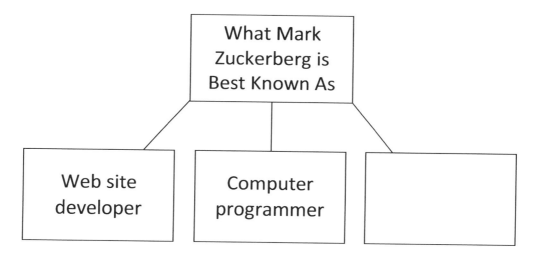

Which of these best completes the web?

    Ⓐ   Teacher

    Ⓑ   College professor

    Ⓒ   Businessperson

    Ⓓ   Fencing champion

STAAR Reading

Mini-Test 3

Instructions

Read the passage. The passage is followed by questions.

Read each question carefully. Then select the best answer. Fill in the circle for the correct answer.

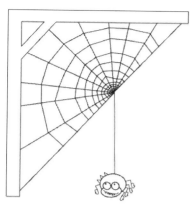
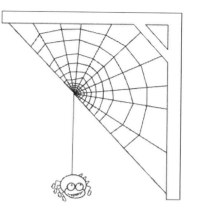

Spinning the Spider's Web

The spider spins his silken web,
In the corner of my home,
He weaves it for his family,
One teeny space their own.

I watch him as he toils,
Through the hours of the day,
Spinning as the summer burns,
Forever building come what may.

And when his web is broken,
He never sheds a tear,
He simply spins and starts again,
And keeps his loved ones near.

This small kingdom is his castle,
And a tiny place to rest,
Although some may beg to differ,
He builds his home to be the best.

He goes about his business,
And does not seek to pry or scare,
He means no harm to those around him,
To cross your path, he wouldn't dare.

The spider just keeps on spinning,
His winding, silken web,
Building homes amongst the darkness,
Keeping family in good stead.

So next time you see the spider,
Spinning webs inside your home,
Think how hard he has to toil,
Without a single word or moan.

1 Read this line from the poem.

I watch him as he toils,

What does the word <u>toils</u> mean?

Ⓐ   Works

Ⓑ   Spins

Ⓒ   Struggles

Ⓓ   Plays

2 Read this line from the poem.

One teeny space their own.

Which word means the opposite of <u>teeny</u>?

Ⓐ   Special

Ⓑ   Massive

Ⓒ   Dirty

Ⓓ   Minute

3   What does the poet seem to find most impressive about spiders?

    Ⓐ   That they can live anywhere

    Ⓑ   That they never stop working

    Ⓒ   That they build their own homes

    Ⓓ   That they leave people alone

4   Read this line from the poem.

    The spider spins his silken web,

Which literary technique does the poet use in this line?

    Ⓐ   Alliteration

    Ⓑ   Simile

    Ⓒ   Metaphor

    Ⓓ   Flashback

5   What is the rhyme pattern of each stanza of the poem?

     Ⓐ   All the lines rhyme with each other.

     Ⓑ   There are two pairs of rhyming lines.

     Ⓒ   The second and fourth lines rhyme.

     Ⓓ   None of the lines rhyme.

6   What type of poem is "Spinning the Spider's Web"?

     Ⓐ   Rhyming

     Ⓑ   Free verse

     Ⓒ   Limerick

     Ⓓ   Sonnet

Grade 6 Practice Test Book

7   Which statement would the poet most likely agree with?

    Ⓐ   People should make their own homes like spiders do.

    Ⓑ   People should keep their homes free from spider webs.

    Ⓒ   People should be aware of the dangers of spiders.

    Ⓓ   People should leave spiders alone.

8   Read this line from the poem.

To cross your path, he wouldn't dare.

What does the phrase "cross your path" refer to?

    Ⓐ   Scaring someone

    Ⓑ   Running into someone

    Ⓒ   Stealing from someone

    Ⓓ   Arguing with someone

STAAR Reading

Mini-Test 4

Instructions

Read the passage. The passage is followed by questions.

Read each question carefully. Then select the best answer. Fill in the circle for the correct answer.

Writing a Short Story
By Kevin Baker

 Writing a short story is a popular and satisfying hobby for a lot of people. It is also an excellent way to express creative thoughts. Writing a good story is not easy, but it is certainly worth the effort. Here are the steps to take to write a good story.

Step 1

Every story starts with an idea. Start by thinking about the things that you enjoy. These activities are excellent subjects to base your stories on. Other ideas can come from thinking about subjects that you'd like to know more about.

Step 2

Once you have an idea, you can then decide who your main characters are going to be. Consider having both a hero and a villain in your story. This will help to keep your readers interested. A hero is also known as a protagonist, while a villain is known as an antagonist. You'll also need to think of the best location for your story to take place.

Step 3

Before you start writing, you need to plan your story. Most writers plan their stories by creating an outline. An outline is like an overview of the story. It should describe the main events that occur. Your story should have a beginning, a middle, and an end. This will help anyone who reads the story to follow its events.

Step 4

Now that you have your outline, it is time to start writing. Follow your outline and write your story. At this point, your story does not have to be perfect. You will go back and improve it later.

Step 5

The story you have written is your first draft. The next step is to read through it and revise it. Here are some questions to help you decide what might need to be changed:

- Are the events that happen clear?
- Is the story interesting?
- Have I described the characters well?
- Can I use better descriptions to make it more exciting?
- Have I left out any important points?
- Is the start of the story good enough to get the reader interested?
- Would the ending leave the reader feeling satisfied?

Keep working on your story until it is the best you can make it.

Step 6

Once the story is complete, read it in full to ensure that it is well-written and easy to follow. Make sure there are no spelling or grammar mistakes.

Step 7

It is now time to get some feedback on your story. Have others read your story so that they can make suggestions for improvements. Then revise your story again. You should now have a well-written, polished, and entertaining story.

1 Read this sentence from the passage.

> **You should now have a well-written, polished, and entertaining story.**

What does the word <u>polished</u> show about the story?

Ⓐ   It is enjoyable to read.

Ⓑ   It is smooth and elegant.

Ⓒ   It has been well-planned.

Ⓓ   It has a suitable ending.

2 Read this sentence from the passage.

> **It is also an excellent way to express creative thoughts.**

Which meaning of the word <u>express</u> is used in the sentence?

Ⓐ   To send something quickly

Ⓑ   To put into words

Ⓒ   Plain or clear

Ⓓ   Direct or fast

3   Which detail about the author would best suggest that the advice in the passage can be trusted?

Ⓐ   He has kept a diary of his thoughts for many years.

Ⓑ   He has a college degree.

Ⓒ   His favorite hobby is reading.

Ⓓ   He has successfully published many short stories.

4   What is the main purpose of the passage?

Ⓐ   To teach readers how to do something

Ⓑ   To encourage people to read more

Ⓒ   To explain the purpose of writing

Ⓓ   To compare different types of hobbies

5   Why does the author use bullet points in the passage?

  Ⓐ   To highlight the main points

  Ⓑ   To list a set of ideas

  Ⓒ   To show steps to follow in order

  Ⓓ   To describe items that are needed

6   In which step is the first draft of the story written?

  Ⓐ   Step 3

  Ⓑ   Step 4

  Ⓒ   Step 5

  Ⓓ   Step 6

7 According to the passage, what is a protagonist?

Ⓐ The villain of a story

Ⓑ The author of a story

Ⓒ The hero of a story

Ⓓ The reader of a story

8 According to the passage, what should you do first when writing a story?

Ⓐ Decide who the main character is going to be

Ⓑ Write an outline of the story

Ⓒ Discuss your story idea with other people

Ⓓ Think of an idea for the story

STAAR Reading

Mini-Test 5

Instructions

Read the passage. The passage is followed by questions.

Read each question carefully. Then select the best answer. Fill in the circle for the correct answer.

The Inventor

Scott had always been a creative individual. Ever since he had been a child, he had loved to experiment with new ideas. As Scott had grown, his passion had only grown stronger. After attending university, Scott decided that he wanted to become an inventor. He used his studies in engineering to design and produce many brand new things. His friends thought that he was misguided.

"You cannot spend your life as an inventor," said his best friend Luke. "You will never have a steady income."

Luke worked as a bank manager and worried for his friend's future.

"Why don't you reconsider and get a job in the city?" Luke often asked.

But Scott would not be distracted from his goals.

"This is my dream," he said to Luke. "I have wanted to be an inventor since I was a small child. I am not going to give up."

Luke would shrug and leave his friend to his many different projects. Over several years, Scott developed many ideas that failed to become a success. His first invention was a device that was designed to make a car use less fuel as it traveled. This had many flaws and Scott was unable to sell his invention. His second idea was a special motorcycle helmet that provided better vision for riders. This invention received little support from people who worked in the industry.

Scott's friend Luke continued to encourage him to find a different career.

"Scott, you have to think about your future. I am proud of you for trying so hard to follow your dreams. I think it is now time to try something else. If you don't, I worry about how things will turn out for you."

"Thank you Luke" he replied. "I appreciate it. But I cannot stop now. I am so close to coming up with something huge. If I left my designs now, all my life would have been wasted."

Luke nodded, "I understand my friend. Just know that I am here to support you."

Then one day it happened. Scott completed his design of a new wing for an airplane. It had taken six months. Scott's new invention would improve the efficiency of the plane. He presented it to several companies who all loved his idea. After some competition, a company offered to buy his idea and design plans. Scott accepted the offer.

"I knew that one day I would make it!" he said to Luke as they celebrated at his apartment.

Luke felt a little guilty for ever suggesting that Scott should give up.

"I don't know how you kept going all these years," Luke said. "You definitely deserve every bit of your success."

1   Read this sentence from the passage.

> **This had many flaws and Scott was unable to sell his invention.**

Which word could best be used in place of <u>flaws</u>?

Ⓐ   Costs

Ⓑ   Faults

Ⓒ   Benefits

Ⓓ   Uses

2   Read this sentence from the passage.

> **As Scott had grown, his passion had only grown stronger.**

The word <u>passion</u> shows that Scott is very –

Ⓐ   enthusiastic

Ⓑ   talented

Ⓒ   impatient

Ⓓ   knowledgeable

3   According to the passage, what did Scott study at college?

Ⓐ   Science

Ⓑ   Mathematics

Ⓒ   Engineering

Ⓓ   Aviation

4   What type of passage is "The Inventor"?

Ⓐ   Realistic fiction

Ⓑ   Science fiction

Ⓒ   Biography

Ⓓ   Fable

5   The main theme of the passage is about –

Ⓐ   not giving up on your dreams

Ⓑ   making the world a better place

Ⓒ   improving on old ideas

Ⓓ   making time for your friends

6   Which word best describes Scott?

Ⓐ   Foolish

Ⓑ   Determined

Ⓒ   Easygoing

Ⓓ   Sensible

7 Which word from the passage contains a prefix?

    Ⓐ   Experiment

    Ⓑ   Inventor

    Ⓒ   Reconsider

    Ⓓ   Production

8 The table below describes Scott's inventions and their benefits. Complete the table using details from the passage.

Scott's Inventions

Invention	Benefit of the Invention
Device for a car	Reduced the amount of fuel used
Motorcycle helmet	Improved rider vision
New airplane wing	

STAAR Reading

Mini-Test 6

Instructions

Read the passage. The passage is followed by questions.

Read each question carefully. Then select the best answer. Fill in the circle for the correct answer.

A Letter to Mr. Hogarth, Editor

June 15, 2011

Dear Mr. Hogarth,

I am writing to ask if I could do work experience with your company. My name is Daniel Wilkinson. I am 15 years old and currently in grade 8 at school. It is my long-term goal to be a journalist. I am keen to spend my two weeks experience at an established media company. I hope that by gaining work experience with your organization, I am able to begin a long career in the field of media.

I have always achieved good grades in my English studies. I have also written pieces for my school newspaper. Last year, I received an award for an essay I wrote for a local newspaper.

I discovered your publication while taking a family vacation in Miami. I found the *Sunshine Times* to be an extremely fun and informative magazine. I am also aware that you write several other magazines throughout the United States. My aim is to first gain some experience in your offices and understand how magazines are produced. Then I would love to get some experience in the field. I think it may be helpful to shadow an experienced journalist to learn the process of writing. If possible, I would even like to write my own piece for your publication.

I have had an interest in writing since I was a small boy. I especially enjoy producing articles on sport, travel, and entertainment. I was drawn to your publication because they have large sections on each of these topics.

When I returned from my holiday, I researched your company at length. I found that your main headquarters are based in my hometown of Phoenix. Needless to say, I was absolutely delighted! After speaking with your assistant I was convinced that it would be the right place to complete my work experience.

I would not like to cause your organization any problems. I do have other options, but your media company remains my favorite. I believe it would be very helpful for me to spend time with you and your writers. I also hope that I could bring something positive to your publications. I am young, keen, and very motivated to become a journalist. It is my wish that we can help each other to improve and learn.

I have included my contact details for your records. I hope very much that I can carry out my work experience with you. If you need anything further, then please let me know. I can provide references from my teachers if required. Thank you once again for your consideration. Your time and effort is very much appreciated.

Yours faithfully,

Daniel Wilkinson

1   Read this sentence from the letter.

I think it may be helpful to shadow an experienced journalist to learn the process of writing.

What does Daniel most likely mean by <u>shadow</u>?

Ⓐ   Copy

Ⓑ   Assist

Ⓒ   Follow

Ⓓ   Question

2   Which two words from the letter are closest in meaning?

Ⓐ   Fun, informative

Ⓑ   Aim, goal

Ⓒ   Newspaper, magazine

Ⓓ   Delighted, keen

3   Why was Daniel most likely delighted to find that the company's headquarters were in Phoenix?

Ⓐ   He knows that he lives close enough to work there.

Ⓑ   He hopes that the company will provide many people with jobs.

Ⓒ   He wants his family and friends to read the articles that he writes.

Ⓓ   He thinks that the company could offer him a scholarship some day.

4   What is the main reason Daniel wrote the letter?

Ⓐ   To explain his future career goals

Ⓑ   To provide feedback on publications that he likes

Ⓒ   To describe what he has achieved so far

Ⓓ   To convince the editor to offer him work experience

5   Which sentence best summarizes the main idea of the letter?

Ⓐ   *I hope that by gaining work experience with your organization, I am able to begin a long career in the field of media.*

Ⓑ   *I am also aware that you write several other publications throughout the United States.*

Ⓒ   *I have had an interest in writing since I was a small boy.*

Ⓓ   *I would not like to cause your organization any problems.*

6   Why does Daniel most likely include the second paragraph?

Ⓐ   To explain why he wants to become a journalist

Ⓑ   To show that he will take the work seriously

Ⓒ   To explain that he has something to offer

Ⓓ   To show that he would be happy to work for any company

7   Read this sentence from the letter.

> **I was drawn to your publication because they have large sections on each of these topics.**

What does the phrase "drawn to" mean?

(A)   Photographed

(B)   Attracted to

(C)   Curious about

(D)   Impressed by

8   Complete the web below using information from the letter.

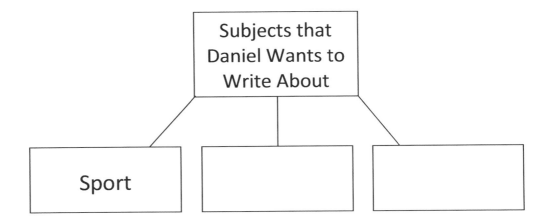

STAAR Reading

Mini-Test 7

Instructions

Read the passage. The passage is followed by questions.

Read each question carefully. Then select the best answer. Fill in the circle for the correct answer.

Beneath the Silver Stars

It was fair to say that Lucas was sometimes mean to his younger sister. He would often play practical jokes on her. His parents used to tell him that it wasn't nice to scare her. He would always say that he never meant to upset her and that he was just joking. The situation was worse when the family went camping together. Lucas would play all sorts of tricks on his sister once the sun had gone down. On one particular trip, his sister Molly was having breakfast and talking about her brother to their dad.

"Why won't he just stop playing his silly pranks?" Molly complained.

"He's just a boy," her father replied. "Although, we could get him back if you want to."

Molly's eyes lit up. Then a smile came to her face.

"How do you mean, Dad?" she asked.

"Well, I think we should play some tricks of our own," he replied. "After all, it's just a little harmless fun. We should wait until tonight and play a few little games."

Molly was very excited at her father's suggestion and thought it was a great idea.

"We won't scare him too much will we?" she asked.

"Not at all," replied her father. "When I was a child my brother used to play tricks on me all the time. It is just something that people do, darling."

By 10 o'clock that evening, it was very dark. All of the family had gone to bed. Molly's mother was fast asleep and her father was awake but quiet in his tent. At about 11 o'clock he began to hear noises from outside of the tent. He undid the zip and peered out into the darkness. He could see Lucas making howling noises from just outside Molly's tent. He chuckled softly to himself and crept slowly out onto the grass. As Lucas continued to howl, his father made his way across and hid behind a nearby tree. Lucas then paused and began to edge closer to Molly's tent. As he did so his father let out a high-pitched howl at the very top of his voice.

Lucas stopped completely still. He half turned but did not want to see what was behind him. His father began to creep up behind him. By now Molly was peeking out of a small gap in her tent. Lucas stared ahead of him and thought about running back to his tent. As he was about to do so, his father reached out and touched his shoulder.

Lucas leapt from the spot and ran towards his tent. Molly laughed loudly as Lucas raced away.

"You see," Molly's father said with a chuckle. "Now wasn't that fun?"

1   If the passage was given another title, which title would best fit?

Ⓐ   Family Fights

Ⓑ   Payback Time

Ⓒ   Father Knows Best

Ⓓ   Good Times

2   Read this sentence from the passage.

Molly's eyes lit up.

This sentence is used to show that Molly is –

Ⓐ   confused

Ⓑ   frightened

Ⓒ   interested

Ⓓ   amused

3   Which two words from the passage have about the same meaning?

    Ⓐ   Fair, mean

    Ⓑ   Pranks, tricks

    Ⓒ   Scare, harmless

    Ⓓ   Peeking, running

4   Why does Lucas most likely make howling noises outside Molly's tent?

    Ⓐ   He is trying to scare Molly.

    Ⓑ   He wants Molly to come outside.

    Ⓒ   He knows that Molly is going to play a trick on him.

    Ⓓ   He is trying to keep animals away from the area.

5   How is the passage mainly organized?

    Ⓐ   Two events are compared and contrasted.

    Ⓑ   Events are described in the order they occur.

    Ⓒ   Facts are given to support an argument.

    Ⓓ   A question is asked and then answered.

6 Which sentence from the passage best shows that Molly cares about her brother?

    Ⓐ *"Why won't he just stop playing his silly pranks?" Molly complained.*

    Ⓑ *Molly was very excited at her father's suggestion and thought it was a great idea.*

    Ⓒ *"We won't scare him too much will we?" she asked.*

    Ⓓ *Molly laughed loudly as Lucas raced away.*

7 Who is telling the story?

    Ⓐ Lucas

    Ⓑ Molly

    Ⓒ Molly's father

    Ⓓ Someone not in the story

8 Where would this passage most likely be found?

    Ⓐ In a book of poems

    Ⓑ In an atlas

    Ⓒ In a science textbook

    Ⓓ In a book of short stories

STAAR Reading

Mini-Test 8

Instructions

Read the passage. The passage is followed by questions.

Read each question carefully. Then select the best answer. Fill in the circle for the correct answer.

The River Bank Creative Writing Group

 Creative writing is a great way of expressing yourself. The problem is that many people never try to write. Many people believe that they do not have the ability. At the River Bank Creative Writing Group, we aim to unlock your creativity.

We are based in Brooklyn, New York. We started our community organization in the fall of 2001. In the years since then, we have brought creative writing into the lives of many local residents. It does not matter whether you wish to write creatively as a hobby or as a way of making money. We have experienced and skilled staff to help you achieve success. We start by teaching the very basics of creative writing. Then we can develop a program that is unique to your skills and goals. This can focus on writing short stories, poetry, plays, or anything else that interests you.

So what exactly do we offer? Well, our creative workshops are known for their quality. Our teachers include professional writers and editors that have experience in writing creatively. We also have guest speakers who attend once a week and share their own advice and experience. These are usually published authors who have achieved success in the field of creative writing. Our guest list is varied and includes successful poets, short story writers, and novelists. Their practical experience is the key to unlocking your creative talents.

We have achieved some great results at the River Bank Creative Writing Group. In 2005, one of our earliest students had their first novel published. They have since gone on to enjoy two further publications and are known worldwide. In 2009, another of our writers had their first poetry collection published. Thousands of our other writers have emerged from our classes as skilled creative writers.

Our classes can benefit you regardless of your goals. If you wish to unlock your creative skill for an exciting pastime, then we can help you. If you dream of being a published author, then we can help you do that too. It has never been easier to unlock the creativity inside yourself. If you have an interest in creative writing, then contact us today. You can speak with one of our staff members directly on the telephone or via email. They are waiting to take your questions!

1   Read this sentence from the passage.

> **If you wish to unlock your creative skill for an exciting pastime, then we can help you.**

What does the word <u>pastime</u> mean?

Ⓐ   Hobby

Ⓑ   Career

Ⓒ   Adventure

Ⓓ   Journey

2   Read this sentence from the passage.

> **In 2005, one of our earliest students had their first novel published.**

Which word means the opposite of <u>earliest</u>?

Ⓐ   First

Ⓑ   Greatest

Ⓒ   Youngest

Ⓓ   Latest

3   What is the main purpose of the fourth paragraph?

Ⓐ   To encourage people to take writing seriously

Ⓑ   To show the success of the writing group

Ⓒ   To describe different types of writing styles

Ⓓ   To suggest that getting published is easy

4   What does the picture at the end of the passage most likely symbolize?

Ⓐ   How long the writing group has existed for

Ⓑ   How much of an achievement writing a book could be

Ⓒ   How the teachers at the group are very experienced

Ⓓ   How the writing group offers a range of services

5   From the information in the passage, the reader can conclude that the writing group –

    Ⓐ   is mainly for young writers

    Ⓑ   offers the services for free

    Ⓒ   is suited to all types of writers

    Ⓓ   considers publishing writers' works

6   The passage was probably written mainly to –

    Ⓐ   encourage people to attend the writing group's classes

    Ⓑ   highlight the benefits of creative writing

    Ⓒ   describe the history of the creative writing group

    Ⓓ   convince successful writers to be guest speakers

7   Which sentence from the passage is a fact?

   Ⓐ   *Creative writing is a great way of expressing yourself.*

   Ⓑ   *We started our community organization in the fall of 2001.*

   Ⓒ   *Their practical experience is the key to unlocking your creative talents.*

   Ⓓ   *It has never been easier to unlock the creativity inside yourself.*

8   Which word best describes the tone of the passage?

   Ⓐ   Comforting

   Ⓑ   Straightforward

   Ⓒ   Encouraging

   Ⓓ   Modest

Section 2
Vocabulary Quizzes

INTRODUCTION TO THE VOCABULARY QUIZZES
For Parents, Teachers, and Tutors

How Vocabulary is Assessed by the State of Texas

The STAAR Reading test includes multiple-choice questions that assess vocabulary skills. These questions follow each passage and are mixed in with the reading comprehension questions.

These questions require students to complete the following tasks:
- identify word meanings
- analyze word meanings in context
- use words with multiple meanings
- understand shades of meaning
- understand and use suffixes
- understand and use prefixes
- understand and use Greek and Latin roots
- identify antonyms (words that have opposite meanings)
- identify synonyms (words that have the same meaning)

About the Vocabulary Quizzes

This section of the practice test book contains six quizzes. Each quiz tests one vocabulary skill that is covered on the state test.

This section of the book covers all of the vocabulary skills assessed on the STAAR Reading test. The aim of the quizzes is to help ensure that students have all the vocabulary skills that they will need for the STAAR Reading test.

If students can master this section of the book, they will be ready to answer the vocabulary questions.

Quiz 1: Identify Word Meanings

1   What does the word <u>notify</u> mean in the sentence below?

When Les saw the problem, he decided to notify his boss.

   Ⓐ   Alarm

   Ⓑ   Inform

   Ⓒ   Write

   Ⓓ   Blame

2   If Darius is trying to <u>conceal</u> the truth, what is he doing?

   Ⓐ   Hiding it

   Ⓑ   Exaggerating it

   Ⓒ   Ignoring it

   Ⓓ   Inventing it

3   What does the word <u>circular</u> describe about the table?

The oak table was smooth, heavy, and circular.

   Ⓐ   What it is made of

   Ⓑ   What it is used for

   Ⓒ   What it feels like

   Ⓓ   What shape it is

Quiz 1: Identify Word Meanings

4   If Samuel is <u>pruning</u> the hedges, what is he doing?

    Ⓐ   Watering them

    Ⓑ   Cutting them

    Ⓒ   Planting them

    Ⓓ   Weeding them

5   What does the word <u>profession</u> mean in the sentence below?

Li hoped that playing golf might one day be her profession.

    Ⓐ   Career

    Ⓑ   Hobby

    Ⓒ   Talent

    Ⓓ   Dream

6   What does the word <u>jagged</u> mean?

The jagged edges of the rocks hurt Greg's feet.

    Ⓐ   Hidden

    Ⓑ   Strong

    Ⓒ   Pointy

    Ⓓ   Slippery

Quiz 2: Analyze Word Meanings

1   If someone is told to <u>beware</u>, they are being –

    Ⓐ   thanked

    Ⓑ   warned

    Ⓒ   questioned

    Ⓓ   scolded

2   In which sentence does <u>jam</u> mean the same as below?

Connor tried to jam all the clothes into the bag.

    Ⓐ   The photocopier beeped because it had a jam.

    Ⓑ   Joy was late to work because of a traffic jam.

    Ⓒ   Kimmy had to jam on the brakes to stop in time.

    Ⓓ   Steve couldn't jam the sleeping bag back into its case.

3   What does the word <u>post</u> mean in the sentence?

Jorge decided to post his report card to his grandmother.

    Ⓐ   To send by mail

    Ⓑ   To score points

    Ⓒ   To display something

    Ⓓ   To place text on a web site

Quiz 2: Analyze Word Meanings

4   How is <u>gripping</u> an object different from <u>holding</u> it?

    Ⓐ   The object is held tightly.

    Ⓑ   The object is heavy.

    Ⓒ   The object is important.

    Ⓓ   The object is held easily.

5   Which word can be used to complete both sentences?

> **The _____ profit of the company is lower than last year.**
> **The fisherman pulled up his _____ to see what he had.**

    Ⓐ   catch

    Ⓑ   annual

    Ⓒ   net

    Ⓓ   line

6   Why does the author use the word <u>snapped</u> in the sentence?

> **Miss Rivera snapped and started yelling.**

    Ⓐ   To show that Miss Rivera yelled loudly

    Ⓑ   To show that Miss Rivera became angry suddenly

    Ⓒ   To show that Miss Rivera hurt herself

    Ⓓ   To show that Miss Rivera took action

Quiz 3: Use Synonyms and Antonyms

1 Read the sentence below.

The water trickled down the rocks.

Which word is closest in meaning to <u>trickled</u>?

- Ⓐ Rushed
- Ⓑ Flooded
- Ⓒ Dripped
- Ⓓ Wandered

2 Which word means about the same as <u>ideal</u>?

- Ⓐ Perfect
- Ⓑ Image
- Ⓒ Thought
- Ⓓ Bargain

3 Which two words have about the same meaning?

- Ⓐ Soggy, smelly
- Ⓑ Monstrous, tiny
- Ⓒ Plea, request
- Ⓓ Quiz, answer

Quiz 3: Use Synonyms and Antonyms

4   Read the sentence below.

Jodie knew that she had not cheated and was innocent.

Which word means the opposite of <u>innocent</u>?

Ⓐ   Safe

Ⓑ   Upset

Ⓒ   Guilty

Ⓓ   Blameless

5   Which word means the opposite of <u>courageous</u>?

Ⓐ   Brave

Ⓑ   Frightened

Ⓒ   Calm

Ⓓ   Cowardly

6   Which two words have opposite meanings?

Ⓐ   Melody, tune

Ⓑ   Permit, allow

Ⓒ   Punch, kick

Ⓓ   Courteous, rude

Quiz 4: Use Prefixes

1 Where would a book's <u>preface</u> most likely be?

Ⓐ   At the end of the book

Ⓑ   At the start of the book

Ⓒ   In the middle of the book

Ⓓ   All through the book

2 Which prefix can be added to the word <u>calculate</u> to make a word meaning "calculate incorrectly"?

Ⓐ   re-

Ⓑ   non-

Ⓒ   mis-

Ⓓ   un-

3 Which prefix should be added to the word to make the sentence correct?

Alison __worded her essay to make it sound better.

Ⓐ   un-

Ⓑ   dis-

Ⓒ   re-

Ⓓ   mis-

Quiz 4: Use Prefixes

4 Mr. Okada and Miss Thomas are <u>coeditors</u>. What does the prefix in <u>coeditors</u> mean?

Ⓐ Without

Ⓑ Against

Ⓒ Together

Ⓓ Double

5 Which prefix can be added to the word <u>equal</u> to make a word meaning "not equal"?

Ⓐ un-

Ⓑ in-

Ⓒ mis-

Ⓓ dis-

6 Which word contains the prefix <u>mis-</u>?

Ⓐ Mission

Ⓑ Misinform

Ⓒ Mister

Ⓓ Missile

Quiz 5: Use Suffixes

1 What does the word <u>purify</u> mean?

    Ⓐ   The state of being pure

    Ⓑ   To make pure

    Ⓒ   One who is pure

    Ⓓ   Capable of being pure

2 Which suffix can be added to the word <u>bald</u> to make a word meaning "state of being bald"?

    Ⓐ   -less

    Ⓑ   -ful

    Ⓒ   -ness

    Ⓓ   -ing

3 Which suffix should be added to the word to make the sentence correct?

    Cody didn't argue because he wanted to be agree_____.

    Ⓐ   -ment

    Ⓑ   -able

    Ⓒ   -ing

    Ⓓ   -ably

Quiz 5: Use Suffixes

4 What does the word <u>successful</u> mean?

Ⓐ Having success

Ⓑ One who has success

Ⓒ Able to have success

Ⓓ Lacking success

5 Which suffix can be added to the word <u>mountain</u> to make a word meaning "one who climbs mountains"?

Ⓐ -er

Ⓑ -eer

Ⓒ -or

Ⓓ -ing

6 In which word is the suffix <u>-ist</u> used?

Ⓐ Assist

Ⓑ Resist

Ⓒ Soloist

Ⓓ Untwist

Quiz 6: Use Greek and Latin Roots

1 The word <u>astronomy</u> contains the Greek root <u>astro-</u>. What does the Greek root <u>astro-</u> mean?

Ⓐ   space

Ⓑ   life

Ⓒ   star

Ⓓ   planet

2 The word <u>botanist</u> contains the Greek root <u>botan-</u>. What does a <u>botanist</u> most likely study?

Ⓐ   pressure

Ⓑ   weather

Ⓒ   cows

Ⓓ   plants

3 The word <u>thermometer</u> is based on the Greek root <u>therm-</u>. What does the Greek root <u>therm-</u> mean?

Ⓐ   Time

Ⓑ   Measure

Ⓒ   Heat

Ⓓ   Theory

Quiz 6: Use Greek and Latin Roots

4 The word <u>bicentenary</u> contains the Latin roots <u>bi-</u> and <u>cent-</u>. If a school is celebrating its <u>bicentenary</u>, it is –

   Ⓐ   two years old

   Ⓑ   one hundred years old

   Ⓒ   two hundred years old

   Ⓓ   one thousand years old

5 The Latin root <u>verb-</u> is used in the word <u>verbal</u>. What does the Latin root <u>verb-</u> mean?

   Ⓐ   Writing

   Ⓑ   Thought

   Ⓒ   Word

   Ⓓ   Sound

6 The word <u>transatlantic</u> contains the Latin root <u>trans-</u>. Based on this, a <u>transatlantic</u> flight is best defined as one that goes –

   Ⓐ   across the Atlantic

   Ⓑ   beyond the Atlantic

   Ⓒ   within the Atlanic

   Ⓓ   near the Atlantic

Section 3
STAAR Reading
Practice Test

INTRODUCTION TO THE READING PRACTICE TEST
For Parents, Teachers, and Tutors

How Reading is Assessed by the State of Texas

The STAAR Reading test assesses reading skills by having students read passages and answer reading comprehension questions about the passages. On the STAAR Reading test, students read 6 to 7 passages and answer a total of 48 multiple-choice questions. Students are given 4 hours to complete the test.

About the STAAR Reading Practice Test

This section of the book contains a practice test just like the real STAAR Reading test. It has 7 passages and a total of 48 multiple-choice questions. The questions cover all the skills tested on the STAAR Reading test, and have the same formats. In short, taking this practice test is just like taking the real STAAR test.

Students are given 4 hours to complete the real STAAR Reading test. You can use the same time limit, or you can choose not to time the test. If using a 4-hour time limit, it is recommended that the student be given a 5 to 10 minute break each hour.

Students complete the STAAR Reading test by marking their answers on an answer sheet. An optional answer sheet is included in the back of the book.

Reading Skills

The STAAR Reading test given by the state of Texas tests a specific set of skills. The full answer key at the end of the book identifies what skill each question is testing.

There are also key reading skills that students will need to understand to master the STAAR Reading test. The answer key includes additional information on these key skills so you can help the student gain understanding.

STAAR Reading

Practice Test

Instructions

Read the passages. Each passage is followed by questions.

Read each question carefully. Then select the best answer. Fill in the circle for the correct answer.

How to Revise

When you revise, you go over what you have learned. Revising is an important process. It helps you learn, remember, and apply what you know. It is also a good idea to revise before quizzes and exams. This will help keep material fresh in your mind. Here are some tips on how to revise well.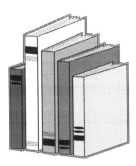

Find Your Place

To revise for an exam, you must first find a quiet and relaxing environment. Somewhere you feel most comfortable works best. It should be in a place where you will not be disturbed or distracted.

Get Set Up

Gather your books and keep them neatly organized along with your papers and stationary. It is also wise to have a fully working Internet connection handy. This helps you to access information that will help you with your studies. You can then start revising by reading your textbooks and making notes to help you learn.

Take Your Time

It's a good idea to make revising part of your weekly routine. The best way to do this is to study every school day. You should set a time each day that you study. You should take care to make sure that you do not revise for too long. Study for a set amount of time so that you can maintain your concentration. Make sure you study for no more than 2 hours at a time, and that you take regular breaks every half hour or so. This will keep you fresh and able to take in information.

Stay Organized

It can be very helpful to set up a system so you are organized. If you are taking notes, file them by subject, topic, and date. That way when you have a quiz or exam, you can easily find the right notes to study to help you prepare.

Check Your Progress

At the end of every revision session, review your notes carefully so that you can be sure that you have understood what you have learned. You may also consider writing out revision cards. You can then use these as a summary of the subjects that you have studied.

1   Read this sentence from the passage.

> **It's a good idea to make revising part of your weekly routine.**

What does the word <u>routine</u> mean?

    Ⓐ   Something you do rarely

    Ⓑ   A regular habit

    Ⓒ   Something that is checked often

    Ⓓ   A process of taking notes

2   According to the passage, why should you take regular breaks when revising?

    Ⓐ   So you do not harm your eyes

    Ⓑ   So you remain focused

    Ⓒ   So you can change to a different subject

    Ⓓ   So you can stay organized

3   Under which heading is information provided about where it is best to study?

    Ⓐ   Find Your Place

    Ⓑ   Get Set Up

    Ⓒ   Take Your Time

    Ⓓ   Stay Organized

4   Read this sentence from the passage.

This will help keep material fresh in your mind.

As it is used in the sentence, the word <u>fresh</u> refers to the material being –

    Ⓐ   strong

    Ⓑ   unused

    Ⓒ   clear

    Ⓓ   clean

5   The table below summarizes advice that the author gives. Complete the table using details from the passage.

Advice for Studying

Where to study	Somewhere quiet
How often to study	Every school day
How long to study for	

6   Why does the author most likely use subheadings in the passage?

   Ⓐ   To encourage students to revise often

   Ⓑ   To describe events in the order they occur

   Ⓒ   To divide the passage into different topics

   Ⓓ   To separate facts from opinions

7   Read these sentences from the passage.

> **You may also consider writing out revision cards. You can then use these as a summary of the subjects that you have studied.**

In which situation would the revision cards you have created be most useful?

Ⓐ   When you have been given an essay to write on a new topic

Ⓑ   When you have an exam the next day

Ⓒ   When you are writing a short story for a contest

Ⓓ   When you are making a science fair project

Little White Lily
By George Macdonald

Little White Lily
Sat by a stone,
Drooping and waiting
Till the sun shone.

Little White Lily
Sunshine has fed;
Little White Lily
Is lifting her head.

Little White Lily
Said: "It is good
Little White Lily's
Clothing and food."

Little White Lily
Dressed like a bride!
Shining with whiteness,
And crowned beside!

Little White Lily
Drooping with pain,
Waiting and waiting
For the wet rain.

Little White Lily
Holdeth her cup;
Rain is fast falling
And filling it up.

Little White Lily
Said: "Good again,
When I am thirsty
To have the nice rain.

Now I am stronger,
Now I am cool;
Heat cannot burn me,
My veins are so full."

Little White Lily
Smells very sweet;
On her head sunshine,
Rain at her feet.

Thanks to the sunshine,
Thanks to the rain,
Little White Lily
Is happy again.

8   Read these lines from the poem.

Little White Lily
Is happy again.

Which literary device does the poet use in these lines?

Ⓐ   Simile

Ⓑ   Metaphor

Ⓒ   Personification

Ⓓ   Hyperbole

9   Based on the poem, what is most important to the lily?

Ⓐ   Having water

Ⓑ   Smelling nice

Ⓒ   Being appreciated

Ⓓ   Getting shelter

10   What is the rhyme pattern of each stanza of the poem?

   (A)   The second and fourth lines rhyme.

   (B)   There are two pairs of rhyming lines.

   (C)   The first and last lines rhyme.

   (D)   None of the lines rhyme.

11   Which line from the poem contains alliteration?

   (A)   *Drooping and waiting*

   (B)   *Sunshine has fed;*

   (C)   *Shining with whiteness,*

   (D)   *Rain is fast falling*

12   Which of the following is used throughout the poem?

    Ⓐ   Symbolism

    Ⓑ   Hyperbole

    Ⓒ   Repetition

    Ⓓ   Flashback

13   Why does the poet compare the lily to a bride?

    Ⓐ   To show how special the lily feels

    Ⓑ   To emphasize how white the lily is

    Ⓒ   To explain that the lily is being used in a wedding

    Ⓓ   To suggest that the lily moves slowly

14   Read these lines from the poem.

Little White Lily
Drooping with pain,
Waiting and waiting
For the wet rain.

What mood is created in these lines?

Ⓐ   Impatient

Ⓑ   Sad

Ⓒ   Calm

Ⓓ   Angry

The Super Bowl

The Super Bowl is the deciding game of the National Football League (NFL). It decides who wins the championship trophy each season. It was first played in the winter of 1967 to determine the champion of the 1966 season.

At the time it was created, there were two American football leagues. These were the NFL and the AFL, or American Football League. The winners of each league would play against each other to determine which team was the overall champion.

When the two leagues merged, the game was retained. It has since become a game where the top national teams play each other for the main championship. The Green Bay Packers won the first two Super Bowls played in 1967 and 1968. They were considered to be the best team at the time. Many people thought they would continue to win for years to come. This changed in 1969 when the New York Jets won Super Bowl III. This was the last Super Bowl that included teams from separate NFL and AFL leagues.

The game has grown steadily in popularity since this time. It is played annually on a Sunday. The timing of the game has changed since 1970. While it used to be played in early January, it is now played on the first Sunday in February. The Super Bowl game has become a major part of America's culture. It has even been declared a national holiday across the nation.

The team that wins the Super Bowl receives the Vince Lombardi Trophy. It is named after the coach of the Green Bay Packers who won the initial Super Bowl games. The Super Bowl has emerged as the most watched television event in America. Super Bowl XLV was played in 2011 and drew a national audience of more than 110 million viewers. The Super Bowl is also one of the most watched sporting events throughout the world. Only the UEFA Champions League trophy in soccer is viewed by a higher global audience.

The Pittsburgh Steelers have won a total of six Super Bowls. They stand alone as the most successful team in the contest's history. The Dallas Cowboys and the San Francisco 49ers have each won the trophy five times. The Pittsburgh Steelers had a chance to win a seventh title in the 2011 Super Bowl. However, they were defeated by the Green Bay Packers. It was the fourth win for the Green Bay Packers.

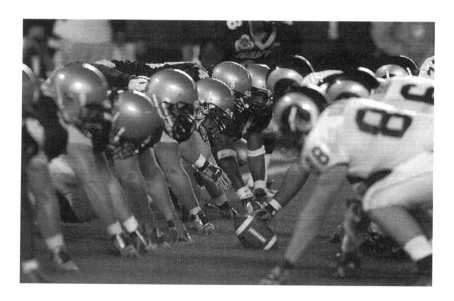

Grade 6 Practice Test Book

15   Read this sentence from the passage.

When the two leagues merged, the game was retained.

Which word means about the same as <u>retained</u>?

Ⓐ   Changed

Ⓑ   Kept

Ⓒ   Improved

Ⓓ   Removed

16   According to the passage, how has the Super Bowl changed since it was introduced?

Ⓐ   It is watched by less people.

Ⓑ   It is played between more teams.

Ⓒ   It is played in a different month.

Ⓓ   It is held on a Saturday.

17 Which sentence from the passage is an opinion?

Ⓐ *It was first played in the winter of 1967 to determine the champion of the 1966 season.*

Ⓑ *The Super Bowl game has become a major part of America's culture.*

Ⓒ *The team that wins the Super Bowl receives the Vince Lombardi Trophy.*

Ⓓ *Super Bowl XLV was played in 2011 and drew a national audience of more than 110 million viewers.*

18 According to the passage, which team has won the most Super Bowls?

Ⓐ Green Bay Packers

Ⓑ Pittsburgh Steelers

Ⓒ Dallas Cowboys

Ⓓ New York Jets

19 How is the third paragraph mainly organized?

   Ⓐ   A problem is described and then a solution is given.

   Ⓑ   Events are described in the order they occurred.

   Ⓒ   Two teams are compared and contrasted.

   Ⓓ   Facts are given to support an argument.

20 Which inference can best be made based on the information in the passage?

   Ⓐ   Vince Lombardi was a respected coach.

   Ⓑ   Vince Lombardi was replaced after the Green Bay Packers were defeated in 1969.

   Ⓒ   Vince Lombardi still coaches the Green Bay Packers today.

   Ⓓ   Vince Lombardi was a football player before he became a coach.

21 Read this sentence from the passage.

> **Super Bowl XLV was played in 2011 and drew a national audience of more than 110 million viewers.**

Which meaning of the word <u>drew</u> is used in the sentence?

- Ⓐ Attracted
- Ⓑ Sketched
- Ⓒ Dragged
- Ⓓ Tied

A New Arrival

Dear Diary,

Today was a very exciting day for me and my family. It was the day that my new baby brother came home from the hospital. He was born yesterday morning at 9:51 am. My father came home in the afternoon and was overjoyed. He weighed 8 pounds and 1 ounce and my parents named him Bradley. My dad says that he is the most beautiful baby. I could barely sleep the night before. I was so excited about Bradley coming home. Eventually, I drifted off to sleep just as the morning sun began to rise.

I woke up as usual today at 9:00 am. I went downstairs and enjoyed some toast for breakfast. I knew that my father was collecting my mother and Bradley at 11:00 am. I watched TV for a while before trying to read one of my favorite books. Whatever I tried to do, I just could not take my mind off my newborn brother. I couldn't help but try to imagine what he must look like. In my mind, he had bright blond hair and sparkling blue eyes. I wondered whether he would understand who I was when he first saw me. My daydreaming was interrupted by my dad's voice. It was finally time to leave.

I headed out to the car and we drove towards the hospital. I couldn't stop talking as we made our way through the winding roads. The short trip to the hospital seemed to take forever. We finally arrived at the hospital. We made our way through the reception and headed to the maternity ward. As we arrived at the doors, I could see my mother at the far end. She held a small bundle wrapped in a blue blanket in her arms.

Mum just smiled as I reached the end of her bed. She looked tired but extremely happy. I just stared for a few moments before Mom asked me if I wanted to meet my brother! I couldn't stop smiling and reached out in an instant. Mom held out her arms and passed Bradley to me. I took him in my arms and held his tiny little baby body close to my chest. As I looked down, he opened his eyes and looked at me. They were the deepest blue that anyone could ever imagine. As I stroked his face he began to smile softly. Dad told me that he looks just like me when I was born. The thought that I was ever that beautiful made me smile. Then Bradley slowly closed his eyes and drifted off to sleep.

Bye for now,

Emma

22   Read this sentence from the passage.

>   **I took him in my arms and held his tiny little baby body close to my chest.**

Which word best describes the tone of this sentence?

Ⓐ   Loving

Ⓑ   Casual

Ⓒ   Lively

Ⓓ   Serious

23   Read this sentence from the passage.

>   **My father came home in the afternoon and was overjoyed.**

Which word means about the same as <u>overjoyed</u>?

Ⓐ   Tired

Ⓑ   Delighted

Ⓒ   Relaxed

Ⓓ   Gloomy

24   Why does Emma most likely say that the trip to the hospital "seemed to take forever"?

    Ⓐ   Her father got lost on the way.

    Ⓑ   She was nervous about seeing her brother.

    Ⓒ   She was excited and impatient.

    Ⓓ   She lived far from the hospital.

25   Read this sentence from the passage.

> **They were the deepest blue that anyone could ever imagine.**

Which literary device is used in the sentence?

    Ⓐ   Alliteration, using words with the same consonant sounds

    Ⓑ   Hyperbole, using exaggeration to make a point

    Ⓒ   Simile, comparing two items using the words "like" or "as"

    Ⓓ   Symbolism, using an object to stand for something else

26 Which of these would Emma probably most look forward to doing the next day?

    Ⓐ   Reading her favorite book

    Ⓑ   Chatting with her father

    Ⓒ   Watching television

    Ⓓ   Rocking her brother to sleep

27 Which word would Emma most likely use to describe her day?

    Ⓐ   Funny

    Ⓑ   Annoying

    Ⓒ   Usual

    Ⓓ   Special

The Aspiring Star

Troy longed to be a professional basketball player. He had loved the sport ever since he was a small child. He was also very skilled and fast on the basketball court. Despite this, he had one small problem. He was very short. His school coach had suggested that he would never make it in the professional leagues. Although he was devastated at first, he refused to give up on his dream.

Troy had several trials at professional clubs but failed to earn a contract. It was then that he attended the training ground of the Los Angeles Lakers. He asked the coach for a trial. As usual, he was refused.

"But you haven't even given me a chance," said Troy.

"Why should I give you a shot?" asked the coach.

Troy paused before he answered.

"Because one day I am going to be the best player in the world and I will be able to help you out," he replied seriously.

The coach smiled at the confidence of the answer.

"Alright kid," he said. "I'll give you a chance to impress me."

Troy took part in a short practice match and was then allowed to showcase his individual skills. He was one of the most skillful players on show and had the will to win to match. The coach was stunned.

"You certainly have a lot of talent for a little fellow," he said. "How would you like to sign on a youth contract?"

Troy agreed and was soon rising through the ranks. Although some players thought he was too short to play, they soon changed their minds when they saw him in action. After two short years, he was a regular for the Lakers and had even won the award as the team's most valuable player. Even with Troy's help, the team was struggling. They were not winning many games and there were rumors that the coach was close to losing his job. It was before a game against the New York Jets that he called Troy into his office for a discussion.

"I have heard that if we lose tonight then I will be replaced as coach," he told Troy. "I need you to do more than play well tonight. I need you to carry the team and win the game. Do you remember your promise before I signed you?"

Troy nodded and smiled at his coach.

"You bet I do coach," he replied. "You bet I do."

Troy went on to play the game of his life that evening. The Lakers won the game and won every game that was left that season. The coach kept his job and led his team on to success.

28   Read this sentence from the passage.

> **Although he was devastated at first, he refused to give up on his dream.**

The word <u>devastated</u> probably means that Troy was –

Ⓐ   understanding

Ⓑ   very upset

Ⓒ   not surprised

Ⓓ   slightly amused

29   Read this sentence from the passage.

> **I need you to carry the team and win the game.**

What does the phrase "carry the team" refer to?

Ⓐ   How Troy will have to cheer on his teammates

Ⓑ   How Troy will have to do extra work

Ⓒ   How Troy will have to motivate the team

Ⓓ   How Troy will have to go against his team

30 According to the passage, what is the main hurdle that makes it difficult for Troy to play at a high level?

Ⓐ   His talent

Ⓑ   His speed

Ⓒ   His height

Ⓓ   His experience

31 Which statement best describes the theme of the passage?

Ⓐ   It is important to keep your promises.

Ⓑ   You can achieve your dreams if you work hard enough.

Ⓒ   Confidence is the key to being great.

Ⓓ   There is no time like the present.

32 What type of passage is "The Aspiring Star"?

Ⓐ   Realistic fiction

Ⓑ   Science fiction

Ⓒ   Autobiography

Ⓓ   Fable

33 Read this sentence from the end of the passage spoken by the coach.

Do you remember your promise before I signed you?

What promise is the coach referring to?

Ⓐ How Troy said he would do anything to win

Ⓑ How Troy said he would never leave the team

Ⓒ How Troy said he would put his all into every game

Ⓓ How Troy said he will help the coach out one day

34 What is the point of view in the passage?

Ⓐ First person

Ⓑ Second person

Ⓒ Third person limited

Ⓓ Third person omniscient

A Pen Pal Replies

Dear Mary,

I hope that you are well. It was so nice to read your letter the other day. I have always dreamed about having a pen pal. It is even better that you live in such a peaceful place and have such a different life to mine. Hopefully, we can learn from each other and grow to be the very best of friends. Life in New York is so busy and it is difficult to find the time to really get to know people. Even becoming close to my classmates has proved to be quite difficult over the years. It is my wish that our letters will let us get to know each other and share parts of our lives.

Your horse Shannon sounds beautiful. I adore animals and am very jealous that you get to live on a farm. I cannot imagine how much fun it is to ride a horse through endless fields and meadows. I would love to come and visit you one day. This must seem strange to you, but I would have to travel miles just to see some farmland. Your siblings also sound lovely. I am an only child, so I can only imagine what it is like to have older brothers and sisters. I bet they look after you and keep you safe. I am sorry to hear that your older brother is leaving for university in England though. At least he will be able to visit you on the weekends. He will probably bring back lots of presents for you and your family!

You would find New York fascinating. I live in a two-bedroom apartment on the tenth floor of our building. New York is very busy, but at times it can be the most amazing city in the whole wide world. At night it is so bright and lively and the whole place is full of things to do. I think I will be able to appreciate it even more when I am older.

My parents say that we may be going to Florida in the fall. I have been there before and it is the perfect place to take a vacation. There are so many children who are our age and it is easy to make new and interesting friends.

I love reading too! I have never read any books by your favorite author Enid Blyton though. I will have to go to my local library and find some. I love mystery books and science fiction novels too. I also enjoy dancing and often enter competitions. I even managed to win a first place trophy last year. My other favorite hobby is ice skating. In winter, I skate in Central Park. In the other seasons, I go to an indoor rink. I am hoping to start entering ice skating competitions next year.

Anyway, I have to go now and do my homework. I have enclosed a photograph of myself and my home address so you can write to me again. I really hope that I hear from you soon!

Lots of love,

Megan

35 Read this sentence from the letter.

> **I adore animals and am very jealous that you get to live on a farm.**

Which word means the opposite of <u>adore</u>?

Ⓐ   Fear

Ⓑ   Love

Ⓒ   Hate

Ⓓ   Admire

36 Read this sentence from the letter.

> **I cannot imagine how much fun it is to ride a horse through endless fields and meadows.**

Which words in the sentence show that it is an example of hyperbole?

Ⓐ   "cannot imagine"

Ⓑ   "how much fun"

Ⓒ   "ride a horse"

Ⓓ   "endless fields and meadows"

37   How is Mary similar to Megan?

  Ⓐ   She lives in the country.

  Ⓑ   She likes reading.

  Ⓒ   She dances.

  Ⓓ   She has an older brother.

38   Complete the web below using information from the letter.

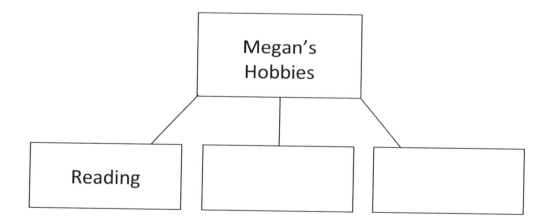

39 Which conclusion can be made based on the letter?

    Ⓐ   Mary and Megan have just become pen pals.

    Ⓑ   Megan has pen pals all over the world.

    Ⓒ   Mary plans to visit Megan in New York.

    Ⓓ   Megan has been writing to Mary for years.

40 Which sentence from the letter is a fact?

    Ⓐ   *You would find New York fascinating.*

    Ⓑ   *I live in a two-bedroom apartment on the tenth floor of our building.*

    Ⓒ   *New York is very busy, but at times it can be the most amazing city in the whole wide world.*

    Ⓓ   *At night it is so bright and lively and the whole place is full of things to do.*

41   According to the letter, where is Mary's brother going to university?

Ⓐ   France

Ⓑ   Florida

Ⓒ   England

Ⓓ   Italy

The Sahara Desert

The Sahara Desert is the world's largest subtropical desert. It covers most of North Africa. Its area is about 3.5 million square miles. This makes it almost as large as the United States of America. The Sahara Desert stretches all the way across Africa.

The Sahara Desert divides the continent of Africa into north and south. The southern border is marked by a savannah known as the Sahel. The land that lies to the south of the savannah is lush with more vegetation. The Sahara Desert features many large sand dunes. Some of these measure more than 600 feet from base to peak.

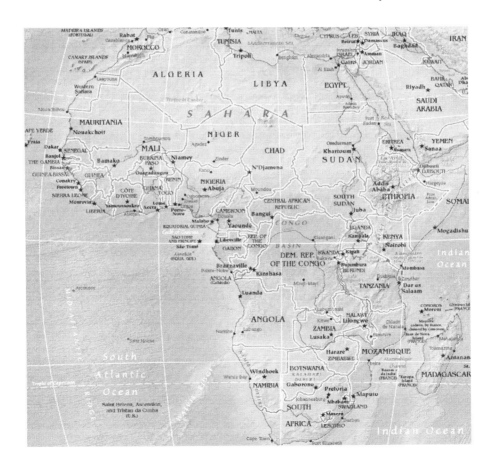

The Sahara Desert has been largely dry and with little plant life for more than 5,000 years. Before this time, it was far wetter than it is today. This allowed more plant life to thrive across its land. Thousands of ancient engravings have been found that show many types of river animals that have lived in the Sahara Desert. These have been found mainly in southeast Algeria. These suggest that crocodiles lived in the region at some point in time.

The climate of the Sahara Desert has also changed over several thousands of years. The area is also far smaller than it was during the last ice age. It was the end of the last ice age that brought a high level of rainfall to the Sahara. This was between 8000 and 6000 BC. Since this time, the northern part of the Sahara has gradually dried out. Though the southern Sahara still receives rain during monsoon season, it is still far less than years before. Some of the tallest mountain ranges occasionally receive snow peaks. The Tibetsi Mountains record some level of snowfall about once every seven years.

The modern era has seen several developments for the Sahara. One of these is that mines have been built to get the most from the natural resources within the region. There are also plans to build several highways across the Sahara. It is expected that one of these may be completed at some point in the future.

42   Read this sentence from the passage.

The Sahara Desert stretches all the way across Africa.

Why does the author most likely use the phrase "stretches all the way across"?

Ⓐ   To emphasize how wide the desert is

Ⓑ   To suggest that the desert is always changing

Ⓒ   To show that the desert is mainly flat

Ⓓ   To indicate that the desert has always been there

43   Which sentence from the passage is best supported by the map?

Ⓐ   *The Sahara Desert is the world's largest subtropical desert.*

Ⓑ   *The Sahara Desert stretches all the way across Africa.*

Ⓒ   *The Sahara Desert features many large sand dunes.*

Ⓓ   *The Sahara Desert has been largely dry and with little plant life for more than 5,000 years.*

44   According to the passage, how was the Sahara Desert different thousands of years ago?

    Ⓐ   It had fewer animals.

    Ⓑ   It was wetter.

    Ⓒ   It had smaller sand dunes.

    Ⓓ   It was home to fewer people.

45   Which of the following is most similar about the Sahara Desert and the United States?

    Ⓐ   Its size

    Ⓑ   Its climate

    Ⓒ   Its uses

    Ⓓ   Its location

46   Where would this passage most likely be found?

    Ⓐ   In an encyclopedia

    Ⓑ   In an atlas

    Ⓒ   In a history textbook

    Ⓓ   In a book of short stories

47   How is the fourth paragraph of the passage organized?

    Ⓐ   A problem is described and then a solution is given.

    Ⓑ   The cause of an event is described.

    Ⓒ   Facts are given to support an argument.

    Ⓓ   A question is asked and then answered.

48   Based on the map, which country is NOT part of the Sahara Desert?

Ⓐ   Algeria

Ⓑ   Libya

Ⓒ   Chad

Ⓓ   Angola

END OF TEST

Answer Key

The STAAR Reading test given by the state of Texas assesses a specific set of skills. The answer key identifies what skill each question is testing.

The answer key also includes notes on key reading skills that students will need to understand to master the test. Use the notes to review the questions with students so they gain a full understanding of these key reading skills.

Section 1: Reading Mini-Tests

Mini-Test 1

The Lighthouse

Question	Answer	Reading Skill
1	C	Identify and use synonyms
2	B	Understand and analyze word use
3	B	Make inferences about characters
4	A	Understand and analyze literary techniques (personification)*
5	B	Understand cause and effect
6	D	Identify point of view*
7	A	Compare and contrast characters
8	B	Understand and analyze the author's technique

*Key Reading Skill: Personification

Personification is a literary device where objects are described as if they are human. The lighthouse is given human qualities by being described as "standing proudly."

*Key Reading Skill: Point of View

There are four possible points of view. They are:
- First person – the story is told by a narrator who is a character in the story. The use of the words *I*, *my*, or *we* indicate a first person point of view.
- Second person – the story is told by referring to the reader as "you."
- Third person limited – the story is told by a person outside the story. The term *limited* refers to how much knowledge the narrator has. The narrator has knowledge of one character, but does not have knowledge beyond what that one character knows, sees, or does.
- Third person omniscient – the story is told by a person outside the story. The term *omniscient* refers to how much knowledge the narrator has. An omniscient narrator knows everything about all characters and has unlimited information.

Mini-Test 2

Mark Zuckerberg

Question	Answer	Reading Skill
1	C	Use context to determine the meaning of words
2	A	Understand the meaning of Greek and Latin word parts*
3	A	Locate facts and details in a passage
4	A	Identify different types of texts*
5	D	Identify the purpose of specific sections
6	B	Identify details that support a conclusion
7	B	Make inferences based on information in a passage
8	C	Summarize information given in a passage

*Key Reading Skill: Greek and Latin Word Parts

Some words are based on Greek and Latin word parts. The word *multilingual* is made up of the Latin prefix *multi-* and the Latin root *lingu-*, which means language. The prefix *multi-* means many.

*Key Reading Skill: Identifying Genres (Biography)

A biography is a story of someone's life written by someone other than the person described. This is different to an autobiography, which is the story of someone's life written by that person.

Mini-Test 3

Spinning the Spider's Web

Question	Answer	Reading Skill
1	A	Use context to determine the meaning of words
2	B	Identify and use antonyms
3	B	Identify the author's opinion or point of view
4	A	Understand and analyze literary techniques (alliteration)*
5	C	Identify the characteristics of poems
6	A	Identify different types of poems*
7	D	Make predictions based on information from a passage
8	B	Identify the meaning of phrases

*Key Reading Skill: Alliteration

Alliteration is a literary technique where consonant sounds are repeated in neighboring words. This line has a repeated "s" sound.

*Key Reading Skill: Types of Poems

- A rhyming poem is a poem with a set rhyme pattern.
- A free verse poem does not have a pattern for rhythm or rhyme.
- A limerick is a poem with five lines. The first, second, and last lines rhyme. The third and fourth lines also rhyme.
- A sonnet is a special type of poem with 14 lines and a set rhyme pattern.

The poem rhymes, but does not have the structure of a limerick or a sonnet. The poem is best described as a rhyming poem.

Mini-Test 4

Writing a Short Story

Question	Answer	Reading Skill
1	B	Use context to determine the meaning of words
2	B	Use words with multiple meanings*
3	D	Analyze the background and qualifications of the author
4	A	Identify the author's main purpose
5	B	Understand the purpose of text features
6	B	Understand written directions
7	C	Locate facts and details in a passage
8	D	Identify the sequence of events

*Key Reading Skill: Multiple Meanings

Some words have more than one meaning. These words are known as homonyms. All the answer choices are possible meanings for the word *express*. The correct answer is the one that states the meaning of the word *express* as it is used in the sentence.

Mini-Test 5

The Inventor

Question	Answer	Reading Skill
1	B	Identify and use synonyms
2	A	Use context to determine the meaning of words
3	C	Locate facts and details in a passage
4	A	Identify different types of texts*
5	A	Identify and summarize the theme of a passage
6	B	Draw conclusions about characters
7	C	Identify words with prefixes
8	Improved efficiency	Summarize information given in a passage

*Key Reading Skill: Identifying Genres (Realistic Fiction)

Realistic fiction refers to fiction that describes events that could really happen. The passage is still fictional, or made-up. However, the events described could actually happen to someone.

Mini-Test 6

A Letter to Mr. Hogarth, Editor

Question	Answer	Reading Skill
1	C	Use context to determine the meaning of words
2	B	Identify and use synonyms
3	A	Make inferences about characters
4	D	Identify the author's main purpose
5	A	Identify the main idea
6	C	Identify the purpose of specific information
7	B	Identify the meaning of phrases
8	Travel Entertainment	Summarize information given in a passage

Mini-Test 7

Beneath the Silver Stars

Question	Answer	Reading Skill
1	B	Identify the main idea*
2	C	Identify the purpose of specific information
3	B	Identify and use synonyms
4	A	Make inferences about characters
5	B	Identify how a passage is organized*
6	C	Identify details that support a conclusion
7	D	Identify point of view
8	D	Identify different types of texts

*Key Reading Skill: Main Idea

One way that identifying the main idea is tested is by asking what would be another good title for the passage. The correct answer is a title that describes what the passage is mainly about.

*Key Reading Skill: Patterns of Organization

There are several common ways that passages are organized. Students will often be asked to identify how a passage, or a paragraph within a passage, is organized. The common patterns of organization are:

- Cause and effect – a cause of something is described and then its effect is described
- Chronological order, or sequence of events – events are described in the order that they occurred
- Compare and contrast – two or more people, events, places, or objects are compared or contrasted
- Problem and solution – a problem is described and then a solution to the problem is given
- Main idea/supporting details – a main idea is stated and then details are given to support the main idea
- Question and answer – a question is asked and then answered

Mini-Test 8

The River Bank Creative Writing Group

Question	Answer	Reading Skill
1	A	Use context to determine the meaning of words
2	D	Identify and use antonyms
3	B	Identify the purpose of specific sections
4	B	Understand and analyze illustrations and photographs
5	C	Draw conclusions based on information in a passage
6	A	Identify the author's main purpose
7	B	Distinguish between fact and opinion*
8	C	Identify the tone of a passage*

*Key Reading Skill: Fact and Opinion

A fact is a statement that can be proven to be correct. An opinion is a statement that cannot be proven to be correct. An opinion is what somebody thinks about something. The sentence given in answer choice B is a fact. The other statements are opinions.

*Key Reading Skill: Tone

The tone of a passage refers to the author's attitude. It is how the author feels about the content of the passage. For example, the tone could be serious, sad, cheerful, or witty. In this case, the tone is encouraging.

Section 2: Vocabulary Quizzes

Quiz 1: Identify Word Meanings

Question	Answer
1	B
2	A
3	D
4	B
5	A
6	C

Quiz 2: Analyze Word Meanings

Question	Answer
1	B
2	D
3	A
4	A
5	C
6	B

Quiz 3: Use Synonyms and Antonyms

Question	Answer
1	C
2	A
3	C
4	C
5	D
6	D

Quiz 4: Use Prefixes

Question	Answer
1	B
2	C
3	C
4	C
5	A
6	B

Quiz 5: Use Suffixes

Question	Answer
1	B
2	C
3	B
4	A
5	B
6	C

Quiz 6: Use Greek and Latin Roots

Question	Answer
1	C
2	D
3	C
4	C
5	C
6	A

Section 3: STAAR Reading Practice Test

Question	Answer	Reading Skill
1	B	Use context to determine the meaning of words
2	B	Understand cause and effect
3	A	Identify the purpose of specific sections
4	C	Use context to determine the meaning of words
5	Less than 2 hours	Summarize information given in a passage
6	C	Identify the purpose of text features
7	B	Apply information from a passage
8	C	Understand and analyze literary techniques (personification)*
9	A	Make inferences based on information from a passage
10	A	Identify the characteristics of poems
11	D	Understand and analyze literary techniques (alliteration)*
12	C	Understand and analyze literary techniques (repetition)*
13	B	Understand and analyze literary techniques (simile)*
14	B	Identify the mood of a passage*
15	B	Identify and use synonyms
16	C	Locate facts and details in a passage
17	B	Distinguish between fact and opinion*
18	B	Locate facts and details in a passage
19	B	Identify how a passage is organized*
20	A	Make inferences based on information from a passage*
21	A	Use words with multiple meanings*
22	A	Identify the tone of a passage*
23	B	Identify and use synonyms
24	C	Draw conclusions about characters
25	B	Understand and analyze literary techniques (hyperbole)*
26	D	Make predictions based on information in a passage
27	D	Make inferences about characters
28	B	Use context to determine the meaning of words
29	B	Identify the meaning of phrases
30	C	Understand and analyze the plot of a passage
31	B	Identify and summarize the theme of a passage
32	A	Identify different types of texts*
33	D	Understand and analyze the plot of a passage
34	D	Identify point of view*
35	C	Identify and use antonyms
36	D	Understand and analyze literary techniques (hyperbole)*
37	B	Compare and contrast characters
38	Dancing Ice skating	Summarize information given in a passage

Question	Answer	Reading Skill
39	A	Draw conclusions based on information in a passage
40	B	Distinguish between fact and opinion*
41	C	Locate facts and details in a passage
42	A	Understand and analyze the author's technique
43	B	Understand and analyze information shown on maps
44	B	Locate facts and details in a passage
45	A	Compare and contrast two items
46	A	Identify different types of texts
47	C	Identify how a passage is organized*
48	D	Understand and analyze information shown on maps

*Key Reading Skills

Q8: Personification

Personification is a literary technique where objects are given human qualities, or described as if they are human. The lily is given human qualities because it is described as being happy. A lily cannot actually feel happiness, so this is an example of personification.

Q11: Alliteration

Alliteration is a literary technique where consonant sounds are repeated in neighboring words. The phrase "fast falling" uses alliteration because of the repeated "f" sound.

Q12: Repetition

Repetition is the repeating of words, phrases, or lines in a poem. The poem uses repetition throughout by repeating "Little White Lily." This line is used in every stanza except one.

Q13: Simile

A simile compares two things using the words "like" or "as." The poet uses a simile by describing the lily as being "dressed like a bride." Brides generally wear white, so this simile is used to highlight the white color of the lily.

Q14: Mood

The mood of a passage is the way the passage makes the reader feel. It is the atmosphere of the passage. This question is asking what mood is created by a specific stanza. The stanza creates a feeling of sadness.

Q17: Fact and Opinion

A fact is a statement that can be proven to be correct. An opinion is a statement that cannot be proven to be correct. An opinion is what somebody thinks about something. The sentence given in answer choice B is an opinion. It describes what the author thinks and cannot be proven to be true. The other sentences are facts.

Q19: Patterns of Organization

There are several common ways that passages are organized. Students will often be asked to identify how a passage, or a paragraph within a passage, is organized. The common patterns of organization are:

- Cause and effect – a cause of something is described and then its effect is described
- Chronological order, or sequence of events – events are described in the order that they occurred
- Compare and contrast – two or more people, events, places, or objects are compared or contrasted
- Problem and solution – a problem is described and then a solution to the problem is given
- Main idea/supporting details – a main idea is stated and then details are given to support the main idea
- Question and answer – a question is asked and then answered

Q20: Make Inferences

An inference is a conclusion that is made based on the information in a passage. The inference is not actually stated in the passage. However, you can imply that it is true based on the information. For this question, you need to think about whether there is information in the passage to support each conclusion listed in the answer choices. All of the answer choices could possibly be true. However, the only one supported is that Vince Lombardi was a respected coach. This inference can be made based on the information given about how the trophy is named after him.

Q21: Multiple Meanings

Some words have more than one meaning. These words are known as homonyms. All the answer choices are possible meanings for the word *drew*. The correct answer is the one that states the meaning of the word *drew* as it is used in the sentence.

Q22: Tone

The tone of a passage refers to the author's attitude. It is how the author feels about the content of the passage. For example, the tone could be playful, sad, cheerful, or witty. In this sentence, the tone is loving.

Q25: Hyperbole

Hyperbole is a literary technique where exaggeration is used to make a point or emphasize the qualities of something or someone. Emma uses hyperbole to exaggerate how blue her brother's eyes are.

Q32: Identifying Genres (Realistic Fiction)

Realistic fiction refers to fiction that describes events that could really happen. The passage is still fictional, or made-up. However, the events described could actually happen to someone.

Q34: Point of View

This question is asking about the point of view of the passage. There are four possible points of view. They are:

- First person – the story is told by a narrator who is a character in the story. The use of the words *I*, *my*, or *we* indicate a first person point of view.
  Example: I went for a hike. After a while, my legs began to ache.
- Second person – the story is told by referring to the reader as "you." This point of view is rarely used.
  Example: You are hiking. After a while, your legs begin to ache.
- Third person limited – the story is told by a person outside the story. The term *limited* refers to how much knowledge the narrator has. The narrator has knowledge of one character, but does not have knowledge beyond what that one character knows, sees, or does.
  Example: Jacky went for a hike. After a while, her legs began to ache.
- Third person omniscient – the story is told by a person outside the story. The term *omniscient* refers to how much knowledge the narrator has. An omniscient narrator knows everything about all characters and has unlimited information.
  Example: Jacky went for a hike. Like most of the other hikers, her legs began to ache.

The point of view of the passage is third person omniscient. It is told by a person outside the story that knows everything about the characters.

Q36: Hyperbole

Hyperbole is a literary technique where exaggeration is used to make a point or emphasize the qualities of something or someone. Emma uses hyperbole when she describes the "endless fields and meadows." The fields and meadows would not actually be endless, but this use of hyperbole emphasizes how large she imagines they are.

Q40: Fact and Opinion

A fact is a statement that can be proven to be correct. An opinion is a statement that cannot be proven to be correct. The sentence given in answer choice B is a fact. The other statements are all opinions of the author.

Q47: Patterns of Organization

There are several common ways that passages are organized. Students will often be asked to identify how a passage, or a paragraph within a passage, is organized. The common patterns of organization are:

- Cause and effect – a cause of something is described and then its effect is described
- Chronological order, or sequence of events – events are described in the order that they occurred
- Compare and contrast – two or more people, events, places, or objects are compared or contrasted
- Problem and solution – a problem is described and then a solution to the problem is given
- Main idea/supporting details – a main idea is stated and then details are given to support the main idea
- Question and answer – a question is asked and then answered

Texas Test Prep Reading Workbook

For additional reading test prep, get the Texas Test Prep Reading Workbook. It contains 40 reading mini-tests covering all the reading skills on the STAAR test. It is the perfect tool for ongoing test prep practice and for reading skills revision.

TEXAS TEST PREP MATH

Help with the Texas STAAR tests is also available for math!

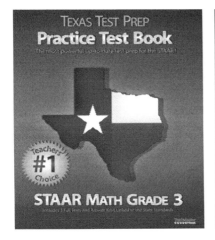 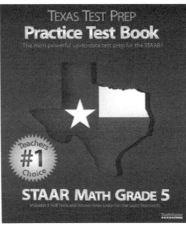 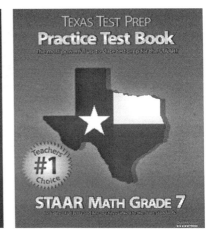

- Powerful up-to-date test prep for the STAAR Math test
- Practice Test Book and Student Quiz Book available
- Covers every math skill needed by Texas students
- Books available from Grades 3 through to 8

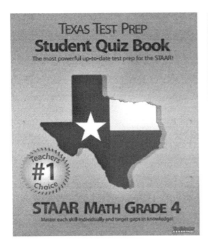  

MULTIPLE CHOICE ANSWER SHEET

STAAR Reading Practice Test

1	Ⓐ Ⓑ Ⓒ Ⓓ	17	Ⓐ Ⓑ Ⓒ Ⓓ	33	Ⓐ Ⓑ Ⓒ Ⓓ
2	Ⓐ Ⓑ Ⓒ Ⓓ	18	Ⓐ Ⓑ Ⓒ Ⓓ	34	Ⓐ Ⓑ Ⓒ Ⓓ
3	Ⓐ Ⓑ Ⓒ Ⓓ	19	Ⓐ Ⓑ Ⓒ Ⓓ	35	Ⓐ Ⓑ Ⓒ Ⓓ
4	Ⓐ Ⓑ Ⓒ Ⓓ	20	Ⓐ Ⓑ Ⓒ Ⓓ	36	Ⓐ Ⓑ Ⓒ Ⓓ
5	Ⓐ Ⓑ Ⓒ Ⓓ	21	Ⓐ Ⓑ Ⓒ Ⓓ	37	Ⓐ Ⓑ Ⓒ Ⓓ
6	Ⓐ Ⓑ Ⓒ Ⓓ	22	Ⓐ Ⓑ Ⓒ Ⓓ	38	Ⓐ Ⓑ Ⓒ Ⓓ
7	Ⓐ Ⓑ Ⓒ Ⓓ	23	Ⓐ Ⓑ Ⓒ Ⓓ	39	Ⓐ Ⓑ Ⓒ Ⓓ
8	Ⓐ Ⓑ Ⓒ Ⓓ	24	Ⓐ Ⓑ Ⓒ Ⓓ	40	Ⓐ Ⓑ Ⓒ Ⓓ
9	Ⓐ Ⓑ Ⓒ Ⓓ	25	Ⓐ Ⓑ Ⓒ Ⓓ	41	Ⓐ Ⓑ Ⓒ Ⓓ
10	Ⓐ Ⓑ Ⓒ Ⓓ	26	Ⓐ Ⓑ Ⓒ Ⓓ	42	Ⓐ Ⓑ Ⓒ Ⓓ
11	Ⓐ Ⓑ Ⓒ Ⓓ	27	Ⓐ Ⓑ Ⓒ Ⓓ	43	Ⓐ Ⓑ Ⓒ Ⓓ
12	Ⓐ Ⓑ Ⓒ Ⓓ	28	Ⓐ Ⓑ Ⓒ Ⓓ	44	Ⓐ Ⓑ Ⓒ Ⓓ
13	Ⓐ Ⓑ Ⓒ Ⓓ	29	Ⓐ Ⓑ Ⓒ Ⓓ	45	Ⓐ Ⓑ Ⓒ Ⓓ
14	Ⓐ Ⓑ Ⓒ Ⓓ	30	Ⓐ Ⓑ Ⓒ Ⓓ	46	Ⓐ Ⓑ Ⓒ Ⓓ
15	Ⓐ Ⓑ Ⓒ Ⓓ	31	Ⓐ Ⓑ Ⓒ Ⓓ	47	Ⓐ Ⓑ Ⓒ Ⓓ
16	Ⓐ Ⓑ Ⓒ Ⓓ	32	Ⓐ Ⓑ Ⓒ Ⓓ	48	Ⓐ Ⓑ Ⓒ Ⓓ

Made in the USA
Lexington, KY
10 October 2014